Vocabulary *Smarts*

Book 1

Series Titles:
Vocabulary Smarts Book 1
Vocabulary Smarts Book 2
Vocabulary Smarts Book 3

Written by

Judy Wilson Goddard

Graphics by

Brad Gates

Anna Chaffin

Edited by

Patricia Gray

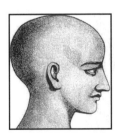

© 2008
THE CRITICAL THINKING CO.™
Phone: 800-458-4849 Fax: 831-393-3277
www.CriticalThinking.com
P.O. Box 1610 • Seaside • CA 93955-1610
ISBN 978-1-60144-172-0

Introduction

The vocabulary words taught in this book are the words that students encounter most frequently in school settings (first 1000 word lists). To give students a deeper understanding of these words and improve thinking and writing skills, students are asked to classify word pairs and then use at least two of the words in a sentence. Simple definitions are given to help students identify meaning and learn dictionary skills.

The book is divided into halves. The first half covers four skills (past/present verbs, singular/plural nouns, antonyms, and synonyms). The second half covers four additional skills (contractions, compound words, homophones, and pronouns).

About The Author

JUDY WILSON GODDARD has worn many hats; she served as a teacher and administrator in both private and public school settings, working with pre-school through college-level students. Throughout her diverse career, she always maintained that critical thinking was important for all levels. Since her retirement, she has continued to promote critical thinking skills by writing books for children. She is the author of many books that apply critical thinking skills to a wide range of academic disciplines. She holds three degrees in education from Georgia State University: Bachelors, Masters, and Specialist.

This book is dedicated to my daughters, Joy and Janet, who are critical thinkers, and to my six grandchildren, with hope that they too will be critical thinkers and that their apples won't always have to be red!

TABLE OF CONTENTS

SECTION 1
Classifications Defined

Past tense and **present tense verbs** are words that tell the time something happened.

Past Tense	**Present Tense**
Yesterday <u>was</u> a good day. ⟶	Today <u>is</u> a good day.
Mom <u>cleaned</u> the house last Monday. ⟶	Mom <u>cleans</u> the house on Mondays.

Singular and **plural nouns** are words that refer to one (singular) or to more than one (plural).

Singular		**Plural**
dog	⟶	dogs
baby	⟶	babies
dish	⟶	dishes

Rhyming words are words that have the same ending sound.

pat	⟶	cat
Dick	⟶	sick
cake	⟶	lake

Compound words are words made by joining two words.

fire + man	⟶	fireman
pan + cake	⟶	pancake
bed + room	⟶	bedroom

SECTION 1

Circle the two words in each group that share a relationship shown in the choice box. Write the letter of the relationship. Then write a sentence using at least two of the words.

Choice Box

A. past tense/present tense verbs	B. singular/plural nouns
C. rhyming words	D. compound words

(score)   (store)   elements

__C__ relationship

The score of the game was posted in the store.

ran   run   engine

_____ relationship

_____

_____

carefully   everybody   exactly

_____ relationship

_____

_____

family   draw   drew

_____ relationship

_____

_____

skin   figure   win

_____ relationship

_____

_____

Definitions

carefully: cautiously

draw: to create a picture with lines

drew: created a picture with lines

elements: forces of nature (storm)

engine: a machine that changes energy into mechanical motion

everybody: all people

exactly: without the smallest difference

family: a group of persons who come from the same ancestors

figure: believe

ran: moved quickly

run: to go quickly

score: a record of points made by competing teams or players

skin: the outside covering of the body

store: a shop where goods are sold

win: to achieve victory in a contest

Circle the two words in each group that share a relationship shown in the choice box. Write the letter of the relationship. Then write a sentence using at least two of the words.

Choice Box

A. past tense/present tense verbs	B. singular/plural nouns
C. rhyming words	D. compound words

square   enjoy   enjoyed

_____ relationship

_____

_____

sight   white   entered

_____ relationship

_____

_____

leave   left   example

_____ relationship

_____

_____

tables   famous   table

_____ relationship

_____

_____

sandbox   handshake   exciting

_____ relationship

_____

_____

Definitions

enjoy: to take pleasure from
enjoyed: took pleasure from
entered: to come or go into
example: someone or something to be followed
exciting: causing a pleasurable feeling
famous: very well-known
handshake: a gripping and shaking of the right hands of two people
leave: to cause to remain behind
left: remained behind
sandbox: a box for holding sand

sight: something that is seen
square: a shape with four equal sides and four right angles
table: a piece of furniture with legs and a flat top
tables: more than one table
white: lacking color

Circle the two words in each group that share a relationship shown in the choice box. Write the letter of the relationship. Then write a sentence using at least two of the words.

Choice Box

A. past tense/present tense verbs	B. singular/plural nouns
C. rhyming words	D. compound words

face   felt   feel

_____ relationship

_____

_____

send   sent   especially

_____ relationship

_____

_____

heart   feeling   hearts

_____ relationship

_____

_____

suitcase   baseball   call

_____ relationship

_____

_____

finally   something   sometimes

_____ relationship

_____

_____

Definitions

baseball: a game of ball between two nine-player teams
call: shout to
especially: particularly
face: the front part of the head
feeling: touch
feel: to sense
felt: sensed
finally: happened at the end
heart: an organ that moves blood through the body
hearts: more than one heart
send: to cause to go
sent: caused to go

something: an unnamed thing
sometimes: now and then
suitcase: what things are put in to take on a trip

Circle the two words in each group that share a relationship shown in the choice box. Write the letter of the relationship. Then write a sentence using at least two of the words.

Choice Box

A. past tense/present tense verbs   B. singular/plural nouns

C. rhyming words   D. compound words

bed   captain   beds

_____ relationship

_____

_____

care   high   my

_____ relationship

_____

_____

rainbow   carry   playmate

_____ relationship

_____

_____

either   blue   true

_____ relationship

_____

_____

ball   expect   balls

_____ relationship

_____

_____

Definitions

ball: a round object used in a sport
balls: more than one ball
bed: a piece of furniture on which to sleep
beds: more than one bed
blue: the color of the clear daytime sky
captain: the person in charge or a boat or plane
care: to feel interest or concern
carry: to support and take from one place to another
either: one or the other

expect: to look forward to happening
high: tall
my: relating to me
playmate: a friend to play with
rainbow: the colored curve in the sky after a rain
true: correct

Circle the two words in each group that share a relationship shown in the choice box. Write the letter of the relationship. Then write a sentence using at least two of the words.

Choice Box

A. past tense/present tense verbs	B. singular/plural nouns
C. rhyming words	D. compound words

beside   express   cannot

_____ relationship

_____

_____

wear   factories   wore

_____ relationship

_____

_____

counted   count   cells

_____ relationship

_____

_____

things   dictionary   thing

_____ relationship

_____

_____

edge   sweetheart   themselves

_____ relationship

_____

_____

Definitions

beside: by the side of

cannot: to be unable to do something

cells: one of the tiny units that are the basic building blocks of living things

count: to name the numerals

counted: named the numerals

dictionary: a book of words and what they mean

edge: border

express: fast or quick

factories: where things are made

sweetheart: a person with whom one is in love

themselves: their own selves

thing: an object

things: more than one thing

wear: to use as an article of clothing

wore: used as an article of clothing

Circle the two words in each group that share a relationship shown in the choice box. Write the letter of the relationship. Then write a sentence using at least two of the words.

Choice Box

A. past tense/present tense verbs   B. singular/plural nouns

C. rhyming words   D. compound words

dry   discovered   why

_____ relationship

_____

_____

contain   main   dollars

_____ relationship

_____

_____

doctors   name   doctor

_____ relationship

_____

_____

break   broke   effect

_____ relationship

_____

_____

change   hit   changed

_____ relationship

_____

_____

Definitions

break: to separate into parts suddenly or forcibly

broke: separated into parts suddenly or forcibly

change: to make or become different

changed: became different

contain: to hold inside

discovered: found out

doctor: a person that treats sick or injured people

doctors: more than one doctor

dollars: bills representing money

dry: not wet

effect: an event produced by a cause

hit: to strike usually with force

main: the chief part

name: a word by which a person or thing is regularly known

why: for what cause or reason

Circle the two words in each group that share a relationship shown in the choice box. Write the letter of the relationship. Then write a sentence using at least two of the words.

Choice Box

A. past tense/present tense verbs   B. singular/plural nouns

C. rhyming words   D. compound words

will   it   hill

_____ relationship

_____

_____

everything   choose   everyone

_____ relationship

_____

_____

build   built   church

_____ relationship

_____

_____

deep   field   sleep

_____ relationship

_____

_____

lead   led   slowly

_____ relationship

_____

_____

Definitions

build: to make by putting parts or materials together (to construct)

built: constructed

choose: to make a choice

church: a building for public worship

deep: having a great distance between the top and bottom surfaces

everyone: all persons

everything: all

field: an area of cleared land

hill: a rounded height of land lower than a mountain

it: that one

lead: to be in front

led: to be ahead of

sleep: slumber, napping

slowly: at a pace that is less than usual

will: strong determination

Circle the two words in each group that share a relationship shown in the choice box. Write the letter of the relationship. Then write a sentence using at least two of the words.

Choice Box

A. past tense/present tense verbs   B. singular/plural nouns

C. rhyming words   D. compound words

five   drive   soft

_____ relationship

_____

_____

could   can   special

_____ relationship

_____

_____

blow   grow   spread

_____ relationship

_____

_____

sound   solve   round

_____ relationship

_____

_____

use   bring   brought

_____ relationship

_____

_____

Definitions

blow: a hard hit
bring: to come with oneself
brought: came with
can: to be able to
could: past tense of can
drive: to move in a vehicle
five: the number between four and six
grow: increase
round: shaped like a circle
soft: having a pleasing, comfortable effect
solve: to find an answer through reasoning

sound: the sensation of hearing
special: being better in some way
spread: to stretch out
use: to put into action

Circle the two words in each group that share a relationship shown in the choice box. Write the letter of the relationship. Then write a sentence using at least two of the words.

Choice Box

A. past tense/present tense verbs   B. singular/plural nouns

C. rhyming words   D. compound words

smell   yet   smelled

_____ relationship

_____

_____

become   speak   because

_____ relationship

_____

_____

people   person   usually

_____ relationship

_____

_____

feet   foot   heat

_____ relationship

_____

_____

find   voice   found

_____ relationship

_____

_____

Definitions

because: for the reason that
become: to come or grow to be
feet: the part of the leg that has toes
find: to discover something
foot: the end of the leg on which the body stands
found: discovered something
heat: the feeling of hot
people: persons
person: a human being
smell: to become aware of an odor by means of the nose

smelled: became aware of an odor
speak: talk
usually: normally
voice: a sound produced by speaking
yet: but

Circle the two words in each group that share a relationship shown in the choice box. Write the letter of the relationship. Then write a sentence using at least two of the words.

Choice Box

A. past tense/present tense verbs	B. singular/plural nouns
C. rhyming words	D. compound words

belong   become   wide

_____ relationship

_____

_____

view   cut   viewed

_____ relationship

_____

_____

wonder   fine   wondered

_____ relationship

_____

_____

fire   wire   while

_____ relationship

_____

_____

into   itself   where

_____ relationship

_____

_____

Definitions

become: to come or grow to be
belong: to be the property of a
    person or group of persons
cut: to sever into seperate parts
fine: a sum of money paid as a
    punishment
fire: the light, heat, and flame
    produced by burning
into: used to indicate entry
itself: that identical one
view: see
viewed: saw
where: at, in, or to what place
while: a period of time

wide: covering a large area
wire: a thread or rod of metal
wonder: to think curiously
wondered: thought about

Circle the two words in each group that share a relationship shown in the choice box. Write the letter of the relationship. Then write a sentence using at least two of the words.

Choice Box

A. past tense/present tense verbs	B. singular/plural nouns
C. rhyming words	D. compound words

clean   year   cleaned

_____ relationship

_____

_____

verb   clear   verbs

_____ relationship

_____

_____

rode   week   ride

_____ relationship

_____

_____

window   class   windows

_____ relationship

_____

_____

danced   value   dance

_____ relationship

_____

_____

Definitions

class: a group of students meeting regularly to study the same subject

clean: free from dirt

cleaned: to rid of dirt

clear: easily heard, seen, or understood

dance: to perform a series of movements to music

danced: performed movements to music

ride: to go in a vehicle

rode: went in a vehicle

value: worth

verb: a word that expresses action

verbs: more than one verb

week: seven days in a row

window: an opening in a wall for letting in light that is usually covered in glass

windows: more than one window

year: a period of 365 days or, in leap year, 366 days

Circle the two words in each group that share a relationship shown in the choice box. Write the letter of the relationship. Then write a sentence using at least two of the words.

Choice Box

A. past tense/present tense verbs	B. singular/plural nouns
C. rhyming words	D. compound words

how   now   war

_____ relationship

_____

_____

weather   took   take

_____ relationship

_____

_____

farms   farm   wild

_____ relationship

_____

_____

anything　　　　afternoon　　　　warm

_____ relationship

_____

_____

may	way	step

_____ relationship

_____

_____

Definitions

afternoon: the part of the day between noon and sunset
anything: an item of any kind
farm: a piece of land used for growing crops
farms: more than one farm
how: why
may: have permission to
now: at the present time
step: a movement made by raising the foot and bring it down elsewhere
take: to lay hold of (grasp)
took: grasped

war: a period of armed conflict between states, nations, or groups
warm: giving off heat
way: a course of action; path
weather: the state of the atmosphere in regard to heat or cold, wet or dry, calm or storm, clear or cloudy
wild: not being under control

Circle the two words in each group that share a relationship shown in the choice box. Write the letter of the relationship. Then write a sentence using at least two of the words.

Choice Box

A. past tense/present tense verbs	B. singular/plural nouns
C. rhyming words	D. compound words

forgive   himself   general

_____ relationship

_____

_____

type   see   saw

_____ relationship

_____

_____

floor   uncle   floors

_____ relationship

_____

_____

paid   pay   water

_____ relationship

_____

_____

they   word   words

_____ relationship

_____

_____

Definitions

floor: the part of the room on which one stands

floors: more than one floor

forgive: to stop having feelings of anger toward someone

himself: the identical male one

general: common to many

paid: gave money for something

pay: to give money for something

saw: became aware by means of the eyes

see: to view

they: some people

type: a particular kind

uncle: the brother of one's father or mother

water: a liquid that comes down from the clouds as rain

word: a sound or combination of sounds that has meaning

words: plural of word

Circle the two words in each group that share a relationship shown in the choice box. Write the letter of the relationship. Then write a sentence using at least two of the words.

Choice Box

A. past tense/present tense verbs	B. singular/plural nouns
C. rhyming words	D. compound words

low   so   increase

_____ relationship

_____

_____

without   yourself   thousands

_____ relationship

_____

_____

show   shown   tied

_____ relationship

_____

_____

dead   head   test

_____ relationship

_____

_____

cupboard   maybe   interesting

_____ relationship

_____

_____

Definitions

cupboard: a closet with shelves for dishes or food
dead: no longer alive
head: the upper or front part of the body (human being or insect)
increase: to make or become greater
interesting: holding the attention
low: not high or tall
maybe: it is possible
show: to place in sight
shown: able to be seen

so: therefore, also, very
test: a set of questions designed to find out a person's knowledge
thousands: very large numbers
tied: to have an equal score
without: not having
yourself: that one that is you

Circle the two words in each group that share a relationship shown in the choice box. Write the letter of the relationship. Then write a sentence using at least two of the words.

Choice Box

| A. past tense/present tense verbs | B. singular/plural nouns |
| C. rhyming words | D. compound words |

sign   thought   think

_____ relationship

_____

_____

man   this   men

_____ relationship

_____

_____

woman   women   information

_____ relationship

_____

_____

candies   bell   candy

_____ relationship

_____

_____

spaceship   interest   racecar

_____ relationship

_____

_____

Definitions

bell: a hollow cup-shaped device that rings when it is struck
candies: more than one candy
candy: a sweet treat
information: the giving or receiving of knowledge
interest: curiosity; concern
man: an adult male
men: more than one man
racecar: an automobile used for racing
sign: signal; mark; symptom

spaceship: a vehicle intended to

be launched into space
think: to call to mind
this: the nearest one
thought: called to mind
woman: an adult female person
women: adult female people

Circle the two words in each group that share a relationship shown in the choice box. Write the letter of the relationship. Then write a sentence using at least two of the words.

Choice Box

A. past tense/present tense verbs   B. singular/plural nouns

C. rhyming words   D. compound words

child   children   desert

_____ relationship

_____

_____

wishes   insects   wish

_____ relationship

_____

_____

today   football   job

_____ relationship

_____

_____

streams   deal   stream

_____ relationship

_____

_____

outside   someone   half

_____ relationship

_____

_____

Definitions

child: a young person
children: young people
deal: a mutual agreement
desert: dry land with little rainfall
football: a game played between two teams in which the ball is moved by running or passing
half: one of two equal parts
insects: bugs
job: a task; assignment; work
outside: a place beyond a boundary, such as a door or fence
someone: somebody

stream: a body of running water
streams: more than one stream
today: on this day
wish: to long for; want
wishes: more than one wish

Circle the two words in each group that share a relationship shown in the choice box. Write the letter of the relationship. Then write a sentence using at least two of the words.

Choice Box

A. past tense/present tense verbs   B. singular/plural nouns

C. rhyming words   D. compound words

talk   terms   talked

_____ relationship

_____

_____

substance   king   substances

_____ relationship

_____

_____

tried   try   indicate

_____ relationship

_____

_____

write   about   wrote

_____ relationship

_____

_____

both   loud   crowd

_____ relationship

_____

_____

Definitions

about: imprecise but fairly close to correct
both: the two
crowd: any large number of persons
indicate: to point out
king: a male ruler of a country
loud: noisy
substance: material from which something is made
substances: materials from which something is made
talk: to speak
talked: spoke

terms: agreements
tries: makes an effort
try: to make an effort to do
write: to set words down on paper
wrote: past tense of write

Circle the two words in each group that share a relationship shown in the choice box. Write the letter of the relationship. Then write a sentence using at least two of the words.

Choice Box

A. past tense/present tense verbs   B. singular/plural nouns

C. rhyming words   D. compound words

already   letter   better

_____ relationship

_____

_____

moon   bank   moons

_____ relationship

_____

_____

army   best   rest

_____ relationship

_____

_____

rule   area   rules

_____ relationship

_____

_____

cats   language   cat

_____ relationship

_____

_____

Definitions

already: before a certain time
area: a particular piece of ground or space
army: a large body of men and women organized for war
best: better than all others
better: of higher quality
cat: a small domestic animal kept as a pet
cats: more than one cat
letter: symbols that make up the alphabet

moon: the earth's natural satellite that shines by reflecting light from the sun
moons: more than one moon
rest: sleep
rule: law
rules: laws

Circle the two words in each group that share a relationship shown in the choice box. Write the letter of the relationship. Then write a sentence using at least two of the words.

Choice Box

A. past tense/present tense verbs	B. singular/plural nouns
C. rhyming words	D. compound words

was   am   inches

_____ relationship

_____

_____

tree   fly   be

_____ relationship

_____

_____

has   hope   had

_____ relationship

_____

_____

when   help   then

_____ relationship

_____

_____

speed   hours   need

_____ relationship

_____

_____

Definitions

am: to be
be: happen
fly: to move through the air with wings
had: owned
has: owns
help: aid
hope: to desire something and expect that it will happen
hours: the 24 equal divisions of a day
inches: a measurement of length
need: obligation
speed: quickness in movement

then: at that time
tree: a woody plant
was: happened
when: at what time

Circle the two words in each group that share a relationship shown in the choice box. Write the letter of the relationship. Then write a sentence using at least two of the words.

Choice Box

A. past tense/present tense verbs   B. singular/plural nouns

C. rhyming words   D. compound words

did   important   do

_____ relationship

_____

_____

park   noun   parks

_____ relationship

_____

_____

understand   listen   underline

_____ relationship

_____

_____

cookbook   located   bookmark

_____ relationship

_____

_____

these   off   please

_____ relationship

_____

_____

Definitions

bookmark: a marker placed betweeen the pages of a book to mark the reader's place

cookbook: a book of recipes

did: finished, completed

do: completing

important: having great meaning

listen: to pay attention in order to hear

located: found

noun: a word that is the name of something

off: away

park: a piece of land kept as a place of beauty or recreation

parks: more than one park

please: to make glad, used in a polite request

these: plural of this

underline: to draw a line under

understand: to get the meaning of

Circle the two words in each group that share a relationship shown in the choice box. Write the letter of the relationship. Then write a sentence using at least two of the words.

Choice Box

A. past tense/present tense verbs	B. singular/plural nouns
C. rhyming words	D. compound words

upon   within   match

_____ relationship

_____

_____

catch   room   caught

_____ relationship

_____

_____

map   page   maps

_____ relationship

_____

_____

brown   town   section

_____ relationship

_____

_____

act   fact   scale

_____ relationship

_____

_____

Definitions

act: something that is done

brown: a color blend of red, yellow, and black

catch: to capture in motion

caught: captured

fact: a thing done

map: a drawing or picture showing selected features of an area

maps: more than one map

match: a person or thing that is exactly like another

page: one side of the printed or written paper

room: a part of the inside of a building set off by walls

scale: an instrument used for weighing things

section: a part that is separate or cut off

town: a settled area that is usually larger than a village but smaller than a city

upon: against

within: inside

Circle the two words in each group that share a relationship shown in the choice box. Write the letter of the relationship. Then write a sentence using at least two of the words.

Choice Box

A. past tense/present tense verbs   B. singular/plural nouns

C. rhyming words   D. compound words

who   shoe   several

_____ relationship

_____

_____

seconds   key   second

_____ relationship

_____

_____

records   fun   record

_____ relationship

_____

_____

lifetime   region   membership

_____ relationship

_____

_____

inside   however   branches

_____ relationship

_____

_____

Definitions

branches: major outgrowths from the stem of a woody plant; limbs

fun: a good time

however: in whatever way or manner

inside: an inner side or surface

key: a device used to open a lock

lifetime: the term of life

membership: total number of people belonging to an organization

record: to set down in writing

records: more than one record

region: a specific area

second: a unit of time equal to one sixtieth of a minute

seconds: more than one second

several: more than two but not very many

shoe: a cover for a human foot

who: what or which person or persons

SECTION 2
Classifications Defined

Antonyms are words that have opposite meanings from one another.

big	→ little
hot	→ cold
light	→ dark

Contractions are words that are shortened forms of two combined words. Contractions always have an apostrophe.

Contractions

they are	→ they're
she will	→ she'll
do not	→ don't

Homophones are words that sound the same but have diffferent spellings and meanings.

flower	→ flour
hare	→ hair
tale	→ tail

Synonyms are words with similar or identical meanings.

big	→ large
sea	→ ocean
laughs	→ giggles

SECTION 2

Circle the two words in each group that share a relationship shown in the choice box. Write the letter of the relationship. Then write a sentence using at least two of the words.

Choice Box

E. contractions	F. antonyms
G. synonyms	H. homophones

rock   stone   suddenly

_____ relationship

_____

_____

sail   strange   sale

_____ relationship

_____

_____

up   down   study

_____ relationship

_____

_____

sea   stood   see

_____ relationship

_____

_____

straight   direct   suffix

_____ relationship

_____

_____

Definitions

direct: going from one point to another without turning or stopping

down: lower position

rock: a large stone

sail: a sheet of fabric used to catch wind to move a boat

sale: the exchange of something for a price

sea: a body of salt water not as large as an ocean

see: to have the power of sight

stone: a piece of rock

stood: in an upright position on the feet

straight: free from curves, bends, angles, or unevenness

strange: odd, unusual

study: to give close attention to

suddenly: happening unexpectedly

suffix: a letter or letters that comes at the end of a word and has a meaning of its own

up: higher level

Circle the two words in each group that share a relationship shown in the choice box. Write the letter of the relationship. Then write a sentence using at least two of the words.

Choice Box

E. contractions	F. antonyms
G. synonyms	H. homophones

wood   each   would

_____ relationship

_____

_____

system   distance   length

_____ relationship

_____

_____

eye   produce   I

_____ relationship

_____

_____

death   life   suppose

_____ relationship

_____

_____

him   suggested   her

_____ relationship

_____

_____

Definitions

death: the end of life

distance: the space between two points

each: being one of two or more

eye: an organ of sight

her: relating to a girl

him: relating to a boy

I: first person of speaking or writing

length: the space between two points

life: the quality that plants and animals lose when they die

produce: bring about; manufacture

suggested: proposed as an idea

suppose: to take as true

system: something made up of many related parts

wood: tree logs prepared for human use

would: past tense of will

Circle the two words in each group that share a relationship shown in the choice box. Write the letter of the relationship. Then write a sentence using at least two of the words.

Choice Box

E. contractions	F. antonyms
G. synonyms	H. homophones

fall   drop   surprise

_____ relationship

_____

_____

work   syllables   play

_____ relationship

_____

_____

stop   end   quickly

_____ relationship

_____

_____

ask   properly   tell

_____ relationship

_____

_____

came   went   quit

_____ relationship

_____

_____

Definitions

asked: to make a request
came: moved closer
drop: to cause to fall
end: the stopping of an activity
fall: the act of going down from an upright position suddenly
play: to engage in an activity for fun
properly: in a suitable way
quickly: respond without delay
quit: to give up or cease an activity
stop: to halt movement

surprise: something that happens without warning
syllables: the division of words into separate parts
tell: to give information
went: moved away
work: the ability to get something done

Circle the two words in each group that share a relationship shown in the choice box. Write the letter of the relationship. Then write a sentence using at least two of the words.

Choice Box

E. contractions	F. antonyms
G. synonyms	H. homophones

some rain sum

_____ relationship

_____

_____

equal even rather

_____ relationship

_____

_____

evening free morning

_____ relationship

_____

_____

fair   just   teacher

_____ relationship

_____

_____

top   temperature   bottom

_____ relationship

_____

_____

Definitions

bottom: the lowest part
equal: same
even: equal in size, number, or amount
evening: the time when the sun begins to set
fair: equal; right
free: not costing anything
just: rightful
morning: the time from sunrise to noon
rain: water falling in drops from clouds
rather: by choice

some: a part of something
sum: the whole amount
teacher: a person who teaches
temperature: the degree of hotness or coldness of something as shown by a thermometer
top: the highest point

Circle the two words in each group that share a relationship shown in the choice box. Write the letter of the relationship. Then write a sentence using at least two of the words.

Choice Box

E. contractions	F. antonyms
G. synonyms	H. homophones

four   provide   for

_____ relationship

_____

_____

group   vowel   consonants

_____ relationship

_____

_____

city   guess   country

_____ relationship

_____

_____

air   oxygen   prepared

_____ relationship

_____

_____

red   power   read

_____ relationship

_____

_____

Definitions

air: the atmosphere we breathe

city: a place in which people live that is larger than a town

consonant: all the letters except the vowels

country: the open area outside towns or cities

for: used to indicate a purpose

four: the number between three and five

group: collection; bunch

guess: to solve correctly by chance

oxygen: a gas that is part of the atmosphere

power: ability to act or do something

prepared: to make ready beforehand

provide: to supply for use

read: to have examined and understood the meaning of a written language

red: a color

vowel: the letters a, e, i, o, u, and sometimes y

Circle the two words in each group that share a relationship shown in the choice box. Write the letter of the relationship. Then write a sentence using at least two of the words.

Choice Box

E. contractions	F. antonyms
G. synonyms	H. homophones

write   possible   right

_____ relationship

_____

_____

close   fresh   clothes

_____ relationship

_____

_____

cried   laughed   ground

_____ relationship

_____

_____

rope   string   nation

_____ relationship

_____

_____

won't   necessary   you're

_____ relationship

_____

_____

Definitions

close: near
clothes: coverings for the human body
cried: to shed tears
fresh: new
ground: earth
laughed: showed joy with a chuckle
nation: a community of people with its own territory and government
necessary: going to happen with no way of stopping it
possible: that may be true
right: correct

rope: a large cord of strands twisted together
string: a cord used to fasten or tie
won't: contraction of will not
write: to set words down on paper
you're: contraction of you are

Circle the two words in each group that share a relationship shown in the choice box. Write the letter of the relationship. Then write a sentence using at least two of the words.

Choice Box

| E. contractions | F. antonyms |
| G. synonyms | H. homophones |

sit   particular   stand

_____ relationship

_____

_____

toward   away   point

_____ relationship

_____

_____

girl   fraction   boy

_____ relationship

_____

_____

ready   first   last

_____ relationship

_____

_____

flat   probably   level

_____ relationship

_____

_____

Definitions

away: distant in space or time
boy: a male child
first: coming before all others
flat: even; level
fraction: a part of a whole
girl: a female child
last: being the only remaining thing
level: even, flat
particular: separate part of a whole
point: to show the position by extending a finger
probably: most likely

ready: prepared for use or action
sit: to lounge
stand: to support oneself on the feet in an upright position
toward: in the direction of

Circle the two words in each group that share a relationship shown in the choice box. Write the letter of the relationship. Then write a sentence using at least two of the words.

Choice Box

| E. contractions | F. antonyms |
| G. synonyms | H. homophones |

few   many   process

_____ relationship

_____

_____

touch   paragraph   feel

_____ relationship

_____

_____

buy   paper   by

_____ relationship

_____

_____

gave   took   once

_____ relationship

_____

_____

form   shape   shoulder

_____ relationship

_____

_____

Definitions

buy: purchase
by: near; at
feel: touch or handle
few: not many
form: shape
gave: made a present of
many: amounting to a large
number
once: one time only
paper: a thin sheet used to write
on
paragraph: a part of a writing
that deals with one subject

process: an ordered series of
events leading to a result
shape: form
shoulder: where the arm joins
the body
took: grasped; captured; won
touch: to handle or feel

Circle the two words in each group that share a relationship shown in the choice box. Write the letter of the relationship. Then write a sentence using at least two of the words.

Choice Box

| E. contractions | F. antonyms |
| G. synonyms | H. homophones |

opposite   all   entire

_____ relationship

_____

_____

answer   solution   order

_____ relationship

_____

_____

summer   other   winter

_____ relationship

_____

_____

complete   done   triangle

_____ relationship

_____

_____

continued   total   repeated

_____ relationship

_____

_____

Definitions

all: the whole of
answer: a reply to a question
complete: whole
continued: to do the same thing without stopping
done: finished
entire: total
opposite: being as different as possible
order: arrange
other: different
repeated: done or happening again and again
solution: answer

summer: the season between spring and autumn
total: an entire amount
triangle: a shape that has three sides and three angles
winter: the season between fall and spring

Circle the two words in each group that share a relationship shown in the choice box. Write the letter of the relationship. Then write a sentence using at least two of the words.

Choice Box

E. contractions	F. antonyms
G. synonyms	H. homophones

turn   course   direction

_____ relationship

_____

_____

passed   tools   past

_____ relationship

_____

_____

get   trouble   give

_____ relationship

_____

_____

there   per   their

_____ relationship

_____

_____

let   allow   picked

_____ relationship

_____

_____

Definitions

allow: to permit to
course: path
direction: a line along which
    something moves
get: to receive
give: to grant; present
let: to allow to
passed: moved
past: a former time or event
per: by means of
picked: selected
their: of them or themselves
    (their clothes)
there: in or at that place

tools: devices used or worked
    by hand or by a machine
trouble: annoyance
turn: to change course or
    direction

Circle the two words in each group that share a relationship shown in the choice box. Write the letter of the relationship. Then write a sentence using at least two of the words.

Choice Box

E. contractions	F. antonyms
G. synonyms	H. homophones

cause   reason   picture

_____ relationship

_____

_____

couldn't   plan   didn't

_____ relationship

_____

_____

earth   world   forest

_____ relationship

_____

_____

thick   plural   thin

_____ relationship

_____

_____

alone   pattern   separate

_____ relationship

_____

_____

Definitions

alone: separated from others
cause: reason
couldn't: contraction of could not
didn't: contraction of did not
earth: the planet on which we live
forest: a large growth of trees
pattern: a set of characteristics displayed repeatedly
picture: a visual image like a photograph or drawing
plan: a method of making or doing something to reach a goal

plural: a form of a word used to show more than one
reason: cause
separate: to set or keep apart
thick: fat
thin: skinny
world: the earth and all the people and things upon it

Circle the two words in each group that share a relationship shown in the choice box. Write the letter of the relationship. Then write a sentence using at least two of the words.

Choice Box

E. contractions	F. antonyms
G. synonyms	H. homophones

he   circle   she

_____ relationship

_____

_____

hear   plane   here

_____ relationship

_____

_____

hold   cows   keep

_____ relationship

_____

_____

quiet   common   silent

_____ relationship

_____

_____

steal   cost   steel

_____ relationship

_____

_____

Definitions

circle: the shape of a ring
common: belonging to or used by everyone
cost: price
cows: domestic animals raised to give milk
he: that male
hear: to take in through the ear
here: in or at this place
hold: to have and keep in one's grasp
keep: protect
plane: airplane
quiet: hushed

she: that female
silent: free from sound
steal: to take something without permission
steel: commercial iron used for building

Circle the two words in each group that share a relationship shown in the choice box. Write the letter of the relationship. Then write a sentence using at least two of the words.

Choice Box

E. contractions   F. antonyms

G. synonyms   H. homophones

found   corner   lost

_____ relationship

_____

_____

can't   compare   doesn't

_____ relationship

_____

_____

hole   copy   whole

_____ relationship

_____

_____

cold   hot   crops

_____ relationship

_____

_____

son   nor   sun

_____ relationship

_____

_____

Definitions

can't: contraction of cannot; not able to

cold: having a low temperature

compare: to examine in order to discover likenesses or differences

copy: something that is made to look exactly like something else

corner: a place where edges or sides meet

crops: plants that are grown to be eaten

doesn't: contraction of does not

found: discovered

hole: an opening into a thing

hot: having a high temperature

lost: misplaced

nor: not either

son: a male offspring

sun: the star around which the planets revolve

whole: complete

Circle the two words in each group that share a relationship shown in the choice box. Write the letter of the relationship. Then write a sentence using at least two of the words.

Choice Box

E. contractions	F. antonyms
G. synonyms	H. homophones

house   home   control

_____ relationship

_____

_____

huge   tiny   great

_____ relationship

_____

_____

like   love   climbed

_____ relationship

_____

_____

mother   melody   father

_____ relationship

_____

_____

hundred   century   from

_____ relationship

_____

_____

Definitions

century: a period of 100 years
climbed: moved up
control: to keep within limits
father: a male parent
from: used to show a starting
   point
great: large in size
home: the house in which
   someone lives
house: a building used for living in
huge: unusually large
hundred: the number after
   ninety-nine

like: to feel an affection for
   someone
love: to feel a strong affection for
   someone
melody: song
mother: a female parent
tiny: very small in size

Circle the two words in each group that share a relationship shown in the choice box. Write the letter of the relationship. Then write a sentence using at least two of the words.

Choice Box

E. contractions	F. antonyms
G. synonyms	H. homophones

idea   thought   minutes

_____ relationship

_____

_____

it's   modern   isn't

_____ relationship

_____

_____

born   members   died

_____ relationship

_____

_____

knew   method   new

_____ relationship

_____

_____

explain   describe   mile

_____ relationship

_____

_____

Definitions

born: given life
describe: to give an account of
    in words
died: stopped living
explain: to give the reason for
idea: a plan of action
isn't: contraction for is not
it's: contraction for it is
knew: understood
members: individuals belonging
    to a group
method: a way of doing something
mile: a unit of measurement
    equal to 5280 feet

minutes: the parts of an hour
modern: characteristic of the
    present, contemporary
new: not old
thought: serious consideration

Circle the two words in each group that share a relationship shown in the choice box. Write the letter of the relationship. Then write a sentence using at least two of the words.

Choice Box

| E. contractions | F. antonyms |
| G. synonyms | H. homophones |

cent   moment   sent

_____ relationship

_____

_____

know   money   no

_____ relationship

_____

_____

travel   move   trip

_____ relationship

_____

_____

late   early   follow

_____ relationship

_____

_____

create   design   gone

_____ relationship

_____

_____

Definitions

cent: penny
create: to be the cause of
design: plan
early: occurring near the
     beginning
follow: to come after in time
gone: left
know: to understand
late: behind
moment: a brief period of time
money: coins or bills used to pay
     for goods and services
move: to go from one place to
     another

no: not any
sent: caused to go
travel: to take a trip
trip: going from one place to
     another

Circle the two words in each group that share a relationship shown in the choice box. Write the letter of the relationship. Then write a sentence using at least two of the words.

Choice Box

E. contractions	F. antonyms
G. synonyms	H. homophones

determined   good   decided

_____ relationship

_____

_____

little   across   small

_____ relationship

_____

_____

chief   president   adjective

_____ relationship

_____

_____

say   body   state

_____ relationship

_____

_____

less   more   blood

_____ relationship

_____

_____

Definitions

across: from one side to the other

adjective: a word that describes someone or something

blood: red fluid that circulates in the body

body: the main part of something

chief: highest in rank

decided: made a judgment

determined: found out or came to a decision

good: based on sound reasoning or information

less: having not

little: small in size

more: greater in amount

president: the chief officer

say: to express in words

small: little in size

state: to express in words

Circle the two words in each group that share a relationship shown in the choice box. Write the letter of the relationship. Then write a sentence using at least two of the words.

Choice Box

E. contractions	F. antonyms
G. synonyms	H. homophones

wasn't   bit   let's

_____ relationship

_____

_____

out   bill   in

_____ relationship

_____

_____

land   sky   believe

_____ relationship

_____

_____

difficult   easy   again

_____ relationship

_____

_____

road   been   street

_____ relationship

_____

_____

Definitions

again: another time
been: existed
believe: to accept as true
bill: a record of goods sold and
    the costs due
bit: A small portion, degree, or
    amount
difficult: hard to do
easy: not hard to do
in: used to show placing within
    limits
land: the solid part of the
    surface of earth
let's: contraction of let us

out: used to indicate an outward
    movement
road: an open way for vehicles
sky: the upper atmosphere
street: a public way with
    property along it (Maple Street)
wasn't: contraction of was not

Circle the two words in each group that share a relationship shown in the choice box. Write the letter of the relationship. Then write a sentence using at least two of the words.

Choice Box

E. contractions	F. antonyms
G. synonyms	H. homophones

least   most   against

_____ relationship

_____

_____

different   began   same

_____ relationship

_____

_____

behind   at   ahead

_____ relationship

_____

_____

sure   as   certain

_____ relationship

_____

_____

meat   among   meet

_____ relationship

_____

_____

Definitions

against: opposed to
agreed: came to an understanding
ahead: in the front
among: in company with
as: to the same degree or amount
at: used to indicate location in space or time
behind: at the back
certain: reliable
different: not of the same kind
least: lowest in importance
meat: animal flesh used for food

meet: to go where a person or thing is
most: greatest in amount
same: identical
sure: not to be doubted

Circle the two words in each group that share a relationship shown in the choice box. Write the letter of the relationship. Then write a sentence using at least two of the words.

Choice Box

E. contractions	F. antonyms
G. synonyms	H. homophones

center   and   middle

_____ relationship

_____

_____

consider   think   another

_____ relationship

_____

_____

night   appear   day

_____ relationship

_____

_____

back   front   angle

_____ relationship

_____

_____

rise   flow   set

_____ relationship

_____

_____

Definitions

and: added to; used to join words
angle: a sharp corner
another: additional
appear: to come into sight
back: at the rear
center: the middle part
consider: to think about carefully
day: the time when there is sunlight
flow: to move in a stream
front: the forward part
middle: equally distant from the ends or sides

night: the time between dusk and dawn when there is no sunlight
rise: to move upward
set: to cause to sit
think: to call to mind

Circle the two words in each group that share a relationship shown in the choice box. Write the letter of the relationship. Then write a sentence using at least two of the words.

Choice Box

E. contractions	F. antonyms
G. synonyms	H. homophones

above   below   kept

_____ relationship

_____

_____

big   known   large

_____ relationship

_____

_____

mountain   valley   learn

_____ relationship

_____

_____

brother   much   sister

_____ relationship

_____

_____

come   go   lifted

_____ relationship

_____

_____

Definitions

above: in or to a higher place; overhead

below: in or to a lower place; beneath

big: large

brother: a male sibling (relative)

come: to move closer to

go: to move away from

kept: held

known: understood

large: big

learn: to gain knowledge by study

lifted: moved from a lower to a higher place

mountain: a large land mass higher than a hill

much: great in quantity or importance

sister: a female sibling (relative)

valley: an area of lowland between hills or mountains

Circle the two words in each group that share a relationship shown in the choice box. Write the letter of the relationship. Then write a sentence using at least two of the words.

Choice Box

E. contractions	F. antonyms
G. synonyms	H. homophones

ship   boat   history

_____ relationship

_____

_____

we'll   wouldn't   ice

_____ relationship

_____

_____

number   numeral   hard

_____ relationship

_____

_____

observe   have   watch

_____ relationship

_____

_____

old   heavy   young

_____ relationship

_____

_____

Definitions

boat: a small craft for travel on water

hard: not easily cut

have: possess

heavy: hard to lift or carry

history: the record of past events

ice: frozen water

number: the amount of something

numeral: a symbol representing a number

observe: to watch carefully

old: elderly

ship: a large craft for travel by water

watch: to keep guard

we'll: contraction of we will

wouldn't: contraction of would not

young: being in the early stage of life

Circle the two words in each group that share a relationship shown in the choice box. Write the letter of the relationship. Then write a sentence using at least two of the words.

Choice Box

| E. contractions | F. antonyms |
| G. synonyms | H. homophones |

oh   include   owe

_____ relationship

_____

_____

remain   nothing   stay

_____ relationship

_____

_____

afraid   fear   ocean

_____ relationship

_____

_____

start   note   begin

_____ relationship

_____

_____

part   piece   full

_____ relationship

_____

_____

Definitions

afraid: filled with fear
begin: start
fear: worry
full: to the complete amount
include: to have as part of a
　　whole or group
note: a brief written message
nothing: not anything
ocean: a whole body of salt
　　water
oh: an expression of surprise
owe: to be in debt to
part: one of the pieces into
　　which something can be divided

piece: a part of something
remain: to stay
start: beginning
stay: to remain

Circle the two words in each group that share a relationship shown in the choice box. Write the letter of the relationship. Then write a sentence using at least two of the words.

Choice Box

E. contractions	F. antonyms
G. synonyms	H. homophones

perhaps   look   might

_____ relationship

_____

_____

wait   major   weight

_____ relationship

_____

_____

poor   march   rich

_____ relationship

_____

_____

to   result   too

_____ relationship

_____

_____

pushed   size   pulled

_____ relationship

_____

_____

Definitions

look: view
major: greater in number, quantity, or extent
march: to move along with a steady regular stride in step with others
might: possibility
perhaps: possibly but not certainly
poor: lacking money or material possessions
pulled: tugged
pushed: shoved

result: something that comes about as an end
rich: having lots of goods, property, or money
size: the measurements of a thing
to: used to indicate movement toward a place, person, or thing
too: also
wait: to remain in place
weight: the amount that something weighs

Circle the two words in each group that share a relationship shown in the choice box. Write the letter of the relationship. Then write a sentence using at least two of the words.

Choice Box

E. contractions	F. antonyms
G. synonyms	H. homophones

pretty   seem   beautiful

_____ relationship

_____

_____

short   represent   tall

_____ relationship

_____

_____

after   before   rose

_____ relationship

_____

_____

each   science   every

_____ relationship

_____

_____

always   sentence   never

_____ relationship

_____

_____

Definitions

after: later
always: at all times
beautiful: giving pleasure to the senses
before: ahead
each: being one of two or more
every: each one of a group without leaving out any
never: not ever
pretty: attractive to the eye
represent: to serve as a symbol
rose: to get up
science: an area of knowledge that is an object of study

seem: to appear to a person's own mind
sentence: a group of words that expresses a statement
short: having little height or length
tall: having great height

Circle the two words in each group that share a relationship shown in the choice box. Write the letter of the relationship. Then write a sentence using at least two of the words.

Choice Box

E. contractions	F. antonyms
G. synonyms	H. homophones

current   return   present

_____ relationship

_____

_____

add   increase   settled

_____ relationship

_____

_____

compound   serve   simple

_____ relationship

_____

_____

correct   sharp   wrong

_____ relationship

_____

_____

around   through   should

_____ relationship

_____

_____

Definitions

add: to build up
around: on all sides or in every direction
compound: make difficult
correct: accurate, right, true
current: occurring in the present time
increase: to make greater
present: current
return: to come or go back
serve: to be of use
settled: placed to stay
sharp: having an edge thin enough to cut something

should: expected to
simple: easy
through: from beginning to end
wrong: bad, incorrect, false

Circle the two words in each group that share a relationship shown in the choice box. Write the letter of the relationship. Then write a sentence using at least two of the words.

Choice Box

E. contractions	F. antonyms
G. synonyms	H. homophones

I'll   often   don't

_____ relationship

_____

_____

over   box   under

_____ relationship

_____

_____

dark   burning   light

_____ relationship

_____

_____

divided   sing   single

_____ relationship

_____

_____

one   bought   only

_____ relationship

_____

_____

Definitions

bought: purchased
box: a container having four sides, a bottom, and a cover
burning: on fire
dark: without light
divided: separated into parts
don't: contraction of do not
I'll: contraction of I will
light: not dark
often: many times
one: a single thing
only: alone
over: across; complete; above

sing: to produce musical sounds with the voice
single: being one unit
under: below

Answers

2. C, A, D
3. A, C
4. A, C, A
5. B, D
6. A, A, B
7. D, D
8. B, C, D
9. C, B
10. D, A, A
11. B, D
12. C, C, B
13. A, A
14. C, D, A
15. C, A
16. C, A, C
17. C, A
18. A, D, B
19. B, A
20. D, A, A
21. C, D
22. A, B, A
23. B, A
24. C, A, B
25. D, C
26. D, A, B
27. A, B
28. C, D, A
29. C, D
30. A, B, B
31. A, D
32. B, B, D
33. B, D
34. A, B, A

35. A, C
36. C, B, C
37. B, B
38. A, C, A
39. C, C
40. A, B, D
41. D, C
42. D, A, B
43. C, C
44. C, B, B
45. D, D
48. G, H, F
49. H, G
50. H, G, H
51. F, F
52. G, F, G
53. F, F
54. H, G, F
55. G, F
56. H, F, F
57. G, H
58. H, H, F
59. G, E
60. F, F, F
61. F, G
62. F, G, H
63. F, G
64. G, G, F
65. G, G
66. G, H, F
67. H, G
68. G, E, G
69. F, G

70. F, H, G
71. G, H
72. F, E, H
73. F, H
74. G, F, G
75. F, G
76. G, E, F
77. H, G
78. H, H, G
79. F, G
80. G, G, G
81. G, F
82. E, F, F
83. F, G
84. F, F, F
85. G, H
86. G, G, F
87. F, F
88. F, G, F
89. F, F
90. G, E, G
91. G, F
92. H, G, G
93. G, G
94. G, H, F
95. H, F
96. G, F, F
97. F, F
98. G, G, F
99. F, F
100. E, F, F
101. F, G